MONSTER JOKES

Michael J. Pellowski

Illustrated by Jeff Sinclair

Sterling Publishing Co., Inc.
New York

Library of Congress Cataloging-in-Publication Data Available

10 9 8 7 6 5 4 3 2

First paperback edition published in 2002 by
Sterling Publishing Company, Inc.
387 Park Avenue South, New York, N.Y. 10016
© 2001 by Michael Pellowski
Distributed in Canada by Sterling Publishing
% Canadian Manda Group, One Atlantic Avenue, Suite 105
Toronto, Ontario, Canada M6K 3E7
Distributed in Great Britain and Europe by Chris Lloyd
463 Ashley Road, Parkstone, Poole, Dorset, BH14 0AX, England
Distributed in Australia by Capricorn Link (Australia) Pty. Ltd.
P.O. Box 704, Windsor, NSW 2756 Australia
Manufactured in the United States of America
Sterling ISBN 0-8069-4585-0 Hardcover
          ISBN 1-4027-0126-8 Paperback

To my brother
Johnny Pellowski

CONTENTS

1. CREATURE FEATURES

What would you get if you crossed a monster with a grand piano?

A Frankensteinway.

Which piece of exercise equipment did a mad doctor invent?

The Frankenstair Master.

Why did Dr. Frankenstein become an auto repairman?

So he could work in a body shop.

MONSTER #1: I feel so stupid. The mad scientist who made me forgot to give me a brain.

MONSTER #2: Would you like a piece of my mind?

The Frankenstein Monster and the Wolfman went to a fitness center and began working out. After a while the Frankenstein Monster noticed the Wolfman was dripping wet.

"Why are you perspiring so much, Wolfie?" the monster asked his partner.

"Hey," answered the Wolfman. "You'd sweat a lot too if you had to exercise in a fur coat."

What kind of werewolf earns patches for doing good deeds?

A wolf cub scout.

What would you get if you crossed a vampire with a bottle of soda pop?
Count Dracola.

When did Mrs. Dracula scold her son?
When he'd been a bat boy.

What creepy group of famous female singers is from England?
The Spice Ghouls.

What has pointy ears and lives in a lake in Scotland?
The Spock Ness Monster.

What kind of soup did Godzilla have when he devoured New York City?
Manhattan Clam Chowder.

Where do chicken vampires come from?
Hensylvania.

Vampires have bat breath.

MONSTER: Help me, Dr. Frankenstein! There's nothing at the end of my left arm.
DR. FRANKENSTEIN: Hold on a minute and I'll give you a hand.

How does the Creature from the Black Lagoon tell time?

He looks at his bay watch.

What does the Creature from the Black Lagoon use to sign autographs?

A water fountain pen.

What would you get if you crossed Count Dracula with the Creature from the Black Lagoon?

A monster that sleeps all day in a water bed.

Knock-Knock!
  Who's there?
Ari.
  Ari who?
Ari afraid of monsters? Absolutely!

MAD DOCTOR: I used lightning to bring you to life.
MONSTER: Oh, what shocking news.

Why did you break up with Cyclops?

He had an eye for other girls.

IGOR: I want you to build a monster 20 feet tall.
MAD DOCTOR: Now that's a tall order.

WOLFIE: Why is that monster sobbing?
IGOR: It's the Grim Weeper.

MONSTER BOOKS

"Dracula's Moving Day"
—by Selma Castle

"Did a Vampire Bite Me?"
—by Chick Yerneck

"How to Become a Mad Scientist"
—by Mike A. Monster

"Am I Afraid of Monsters?"
—by Noah Whey

MAD SCIENTIST: I'm going to send a killer bee after you.

HERO: Oh, stop bugging me!

What is very old and creepy and makes people itch?

A fleahistoric monster.

What monster lived in prehistoric times and drove a very old car?

Tyrannosaurus Wrecks.

What monster lived in prehistoric times and wore plaid?

Tyrannosaurus Chex.

Why don't prehistoric monsters need wristwatches?

Because they lived before the dawn of time.

REPORTER: Are you a vampire or a werewolf?

MONSTER: Actually, I'm a little bit of both. Just think of me as a bloodhound.

FARMER: Last night my cow turned into an ugly monster.

REPORTER: Oh, the udder horror of it!

What's scary, stupid, and has feathers?
  The monster from the Black Lagoonie Bird.

Knock-Knock!
  Who's there?
Ghoul friends.
  Ghoul friends who?
Ghoul friends go out with boy friends.

What toy does a baby monster swing around its stomach?
  A ghoula hoop.

What do smart monsters wear in rainy weather?
  Ghoulashes.

What position did the monster play on the baseball team?
  It was the fright fielder.

What monster owns the New York Yankee Monsters?
  George Frankensteinbrenner.

Why didn't Dr. Frankenstein create a smart monster?

He didn't have the brains to do it.

What did the mad scientist name his dandruff monster?

Flakenstein.

FRANKENSTEIN MONSTER: I think I need a good psychologist. Every time there's trouble I fall to pieces.

IGOR: You don't need a good psychologist. You need a good seamstress.

DR. FRANKENSTEIN: I'm just an average scientist.

IGOR: Maybe that's why you created a C-monster.

What creepy chef cooks meals in a wok?

The Frankenstirfry monster.

What did the lonely monster say to the mad scientist?

"I vant to be a clone."

2. MONSTROUS FUN

MAD SCIENTIST: I created a creature out of cow parts.
IGOR: What do you call it?
MAD SCIENTIST: A Mooster.

What hairy monster lives in the forest of Oz, wears a size 30 shoe and is three feet tall?
Sasquatch the Munchkin.

What monster breaks into vaults and devours money?
Bankenstein.

What drinks blood, has fangs and is only three feet tall?

A six-foot vampire bending over to tie his shoe.

What did the vampire bat say when it saw a giraffe for the first time?

"Wow! Where do I start?"

Why didn't the vampire attack the giraffe?

It was afraid it would bite off more than it could chew.

ROBOT MONSTER

Why doesn't the robot monster ever get upset?
It has nerves of steel.

Why doesn't the robot monster ever get a bellyache?
It has a cast iron stomach.

What is the robot monster's favorite music?
Heavy metal.

Why did the robot monster go to the psychologist?
It had a screw loose.

Why does the robot monster talk so much?
It has a motor mouth.

"What should I do with these oars?" asked Daniel.
"Rodan!"

What do you get if Rodan the bird monster builds its nest on Old Faithful the geyser?
Hard-boiled eggs for a thousand.

Why does Rodan always get up at sunrise?
Because the early bird catches the worm.

At what street corner did the Wolfman bump into Tarzan?

At the corner of Howlywood and Vine.

What's the best way to watch a horror movie?
On a wide scream T.V.

INVISIBLE MAN: I want to audition for the role of the Invisible Man in your new monster movie.
DIRECTOR: Sorry, I just can't see you in the part.

Why did the bald man go to the monster movie?
He heard it was a hair-raising flick.

What monster made a lot of money in the movie business?
Godzillionaire.

How are Dracula and the Wolfman like Hollywood gossip columnists?
You only see them when the stars come out.

ANN: I'm starring in a monster movie.
FRAN: How did you get the part?
ANN: I performed well in a scream test.

DIRECTOR: Count Dracula, we'd like you to play a vampire in our horror movie.
COUNT: Now that sounds like a role I can sink my teeth into.

DIRECTOR: I just made a scary movie about a giant bug.

PRODUCER: What's it called?

DIRECTOR: Flyday the Thirteenth.

What would you get if you crossed a Sasquatch with a centipede?

Big Foot-Foot-Foot-Foot. . . .

What happened to Big Foot when he opened a footwear factory?

He became a shoe business star.

SASK SHOES

OOHHH... THAT'S A PRETTY NICE FIT!!...

Where do zombies go swimming?
In the Dead Sea.

Knock-Knock!
Who's there?
Ditty.
Ditty who?
Ditty see a zombie out there or not?

Why did the Sasquatch go to the beach?
Because it was shore footed.

Why did the mummy go to the beach?
To bury itself in the sand.

Mummies who won't wash can end up in denial.

Knock-Knock!
  Who's there?
Opie.
  Opie who?
Opie doesn't mind a visit from a monster!

Knock-Knock!
  Who's there?
Martian.
  Martian who?
Martian bands make lots of noise.

Knock-Knock!
  Who's there?
Eyelid.
  Eyelid who?
"Eyelid a secret life," said Dr. Jekyll.

Knock-Knock!
  Who's there?
Dispel.
  Dispel who?
Dispel the witch cast isn't working.

Whom did the Frankenstein monster ask to the prom?

His ghoulfriend.

What kind of car did Big Foot drive to the prom?

A toe truck.

Why didn't the Abominable Snowman go the prom?

He got cold feet.

3. GOING BATTY

What would you get if you crossed Count Dracula with a fish?

A caped cod.

What oinks, has a curly tail and bites your neck?

A Hampire.

Which monster chased the three little vampire pigs?

The Big Bat Wolf.

Knock-Knock!
  Who's there?
Doughnut.
  Doughnut who?
Doughnut go to Dracula's castle after dark.

What is Santa vampire's favorite kind of blood?
  Type O-O-O!

What monster eats a lot of junk food?
  Snackula.

What would you get if you crossed Count Dracula
with a monster dog?
  A creature whose bite is much worse than its bark.

What did Dracula say when Sir Lancelot showed up at his castle after midnight?

"Oh boy! A late knight snack."

IGOR: Does Dracula take Amtrak?
GREGOR: No. He always takes a fright train.

What did the vampire clerk shout to the people in the checkout line?

"Okay! Who's necks?"

"Shall we add up all the vampires we know?" asked the student.

"No. Don't Count Dracula," replied the teacher.

MAD DOCTOR: You look exhausted.
VAMPIRE: I am. It's been hundreds of years since I've had a good night's sleep.

Knock-Knock!
  Who's there?
Ivan.
  Ivan who?
Ivan hunting monsters all night.

Knock-Knock!
  Who's there?
Clara.
  Clara who?
Clara path! The monster is coming and I'm out of here!

Knock-Knock!
  Who's there?
Teller.
  Teller who?
Teller not to scream so loud.

What happened when the Abominable Snowman met Dracula?
  Frost Bite.

Why did the girl date the Abominable Snowman?
  He knew how to chill out.

Why did the girl break up with the Abominable Snowman?
  She said he had ice water in his veins.

What does the Abominable Snowman do when people wave at him?
  He gives them the cold shoulder.

What vampire art dangles from wires?
  A bat-mobile.

What happens when Count Dracula bites a fly?
  The fly changes into a mosquito.

Does Count Dracula have good medical coverage?
  No, but he has a terrific dental plan.

What would you get if you crossed a church bell with Dracula?

A dingbat.

What would you get if you crossed Dracula with a PC?

Computer bytes.

Which vampire is really hip?
  Count Dracoola.

IGOR: Dracula is working the late shift as a short
  order cook in a greasy restaurant.
GREGOR: Sounds like a fry-by-night operation.

VAMPIRE BEST SELLERS

"Beware of Vampires" by Donna Bitame

"When Vampires Come Out to Play"

by Dirk Knights

"Do You Want to Meet Count Dracula?"

by Noah Tanks

Who is the leader of the Vampire Ducks?
  Count Down.

What does Dracula watch when he wants to know who's hanging around Transylvania?
  The Nightly Noose.

What does King Kong wear when he barbecues ribs?
  An Ape-ron.

What would you get if you crossed a hornet with a giant ape?
  Sting Kong.

How do you go fishing for King Kong?
  Bait a giant hook with a 2,000 pound banana.

What is King Kong's favorite Christmas carol?
  Jungle Bells!

What do you call the brother of King Kong's father?
  The monkey's uncle.

How does King Kong get into his locked house?
  He opens the door with his mon-key.

Why did you break up with King Kong?
  Because he makes a monkey out of himself.

What would you get if you crossed King Kong with Humpty Dumpty?

A monster that climbs up the Empire State Building, then falls off and cracks its head.

Knock-Knock!

Who's there?

Wendy.

Wendy who?

Wendy lightning strikes the tower, the monster will come to life.

Knock-Knock!

Who's there?

Shirley.

Shirley who?

Shirley you're not afraid of monsters, are you?

4. CHILLING CHUCKLES

What would you get if you crossed a giant ape with a game of table tennis?

King Ping Pong.

What would you get if you crossed Godzilla and the Ruler of the Emerald City?

The Giant Lizard of Oz.

What dinosaur is a witch?
Tyrannosaurus Hex.

Knock-Knock!
Who's there?
Hex.
Hex who?
Hex time use a spell that works.

What does a witch use to grade spelling papers?
A magic marker.

ZACK: I just saw a cube-shaped monster.
MACK: Maybe it's the Creature from the Block
Lagoon.

Beware of the jumprope monster!
It'll make you skip town.

Beware of the giant eraser monster!
It'll try to rub you out.

Beware of the locomotive monster!
It'll Choo! Choo! Choo! you up.

Beware of the warm brakes monster!
It'll make you screech.

What monster steals from the rich and gives to the
poor?
Blobin Hood.

Why did the Blob take an aerobics class?
It was completely out of shape.

What happens when you throw a shapeless space
monster in the ocean?
It blobs up and down.

What's itchier than a werewolf with fleas?
Godzilla with chicken pox.

What seafood does Godzilla like to eat?
Fish and ships.

What would you get if you crossed Godzilla with a skunk?
The world's biggest stinker.

Where did the zombie work at the post office?
In the dead letter department.

Why did the zombie go to the telegraph office?
He had to send a cryptogram.

What would you get if you crossed a zombie with a library?
Dead silence.

Why didn't the mummy take a vacation?
He was too wrapped up in his work.

Why wasn't the executioner convicted in court?
His case ended up with a hung jury.

DIRECTOR: I made a cheap horror flick about a giant stinging insect.
CRITIC: Sounds like a B-movie to me.

MONSTER: I'm taking over the part of the Sasquatch for the monster actor who quit.
DIRECTOR: Well, you have some big shoes to fill.

What's creepy and loves country western music?
The Phantom of the Grand Ole Opry.

What kind of music does a mummy love?
Wrap.

Where's the best place for a mummy to live?
In an old, old, old age home.

AHMAD: This mummy we discovered is very special.
ABDUL: How can you tell?
AHMAD: It's gift wrapped.

What did the Egyptian mummy say to the river?
"Nile see you later."

How does King Neptune keep his home clean?
He has a mermaid.

What monster is very sloppy?
The Loch Mess Monster.

What did the Loch Ness Monster eat for lunch?
A submarine sandwich.

REPORTER: Is the Loch Ness Monster intelligent?
SCIENTIST: I believe it is a deep thinker.

What fish helped work on the Frankenstein
Monster's head?
The brain sturgeon.

DR. FRANKENSTEIN: I can create a monster that has
no brain.
IGOR: That's unthinkable!

Which fish destroyed the city of Tokyo?
Codzilla.

Why won't Godzilla devour the city of Athens?
It has too much Greece in it.

What kind of vegetables does Godzilla eat?
Human beans.

Which country did Godzilla eat on Thanksgiving
Day?
Turkey, of course.

What's green, bumpy and has a monstrous shadow side?

Dr. Pickle and Mr. Hyde.

What's Dr. Jekyll's favorite game?

Hyde and Seek.

What's Mr. Hyde's favorite game?

Hyde and Sneak.

What problem does little Jekyll have when he goes to summer camp?

He doesn't know what name to sew in his underwear.

What did Dr. Jekyll say after he drank a potion?

"I'm not myself today."

5. NOW THAT'S A HOWL!

What's furry, howls at the full moon and bounces?
A werewolf on a trampoline.

Knock-Knock!
  Who's there?
Howell.
  Howell who?
Howell all you like, Werewolf, you're not coming in.

What do you call a metric werewolf?
The liter of the pack.

What would you get if you crossed a werewolf with Santa Claus?

A Furry Merry Christmas.

What would you get if you crossed werewolves with magic lamps?

Howl-A-Genies.

When did the werewolf fall for his girlfriend?

It was love at first bite.

What would you call a hairy monster wearing a wool sweater?

A werewolf in sheep's clothing.

What do you call a tired, furry monster?

A wearywolf.

What do werewolves use to play catch?

A fur ball.

What did the man say as he watched the werewolf run away?

"Hairy back!"

What person do werewolves fear most?
The Lone Ranger. He has too many silver bullets.

What would you get if you crossed a woolly mammoth with a werewolf?
A big, hairy thing that trumpets at the full moon.

What kind of rabbit changes into a monster when the moon is full?
A harewolf.

What dresses like a forest ranger and turns into a monster when the full moon rises?
Smokey the Bearwolf.

Knock-Knock!
   Who's there?
Defer.
   Defer who?
Defer coat of a werewolf is very thick.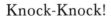

Knock-Knock!
   Who's there?
Derail.
   Derail who?
Derail of a sad werewolf is a frightening thing.

Knock-Knock!
   Who's there?
Decry.
   Decry who?
Decry of the werewolf sends shivers down my spine.

What do you feed a baby witch?
   A magic formula.

What is a little banshee's favorite game?
   Hide and Shriek.

What is a baby vampire's favorite game?
   Batty-cake.

What do you call a baby vampire who is too little to walk?
   A night crawler.

Why is it so easy to take care of a baby werewolf?
It only needs a change when the full moon rises.

What should you use when you change the diaper of a baby werewolf?
Flea powder.

Which letters of the alphabet did the baby Loch Ness Monster learn first?
Its A-B-C-serpents.

Where did the Frankenstein monster go to kindergarten?
At an elementary ghoul.

Where did Little Rodan go after elementary school?
To junior fly school.

Where did Count Dracula earn his college degree?
At night school.

Does Dracula like to take a shower?
He'd rather take a blood bath.

Why did Dracula break up with the lady werewolf?
Every night they fought tooth and nail.

What would you get if you crossed a hobo with Count Dracula?
A trampire.

What would you get if you crossed a manicurist with Count Dracula?
A nail biter.

GHOUL: Why do you look so sad, Drac?
DRACULA: I just bit a duck.
GHOUL: Oh, that's why you're down in the mouth.

Why did Count Dracula buy a pogo stick?
He wanted to bite some kangaroos.

WHAT WOULD YOU GET IF YOU CROSSED COUNT DRACULA AND A . . .

CASHIER?

Count Your Change.

A FOURTH STRIKE?

Count Yourself Out.

AN OPTIMIST?

Count Your Blessings.

CALCULATOR?

Count On Me.

ASTROLOGER?

Count Your Lucky Stars.

What is Dracula's favorite fruit?
A necktarine.

Where do flaky vampires go when they nod off?
To Dracula-la land.

6. (NOT SO) SNEAKY SNICKERS

What monsters can fly?
The ones with airline tickets.

Knock-Knock!
  Who's there?
Iraq.
  Iraq who?
Iraq my brain trying to think of new monsters to create.

MAD DOCTOR: I can't create monsters if I have nothing to work with.
IGOR: Don't blame me if you're having an out-of-bodies experience.

Which skunk was a famous writer of horror stories?
Edgar Allan Pew!

IVAN: I must be going nutty.

IGOR: What makes you think that?

IVAN: I thought I just saw Dr. Jekyll and Mr. Hyde in the same place at the same time.

"Should I conceal myself before the police arrive?" asked Dr. Jekyll as he drank a potion.

"Yes, Hyde!"

GREGOR: Prove that you can fight a monster using only a penknife.

HERO: Okay, I'll take a stab at it.

MAD DOCTOR: I'm going to give my new monster the mind of a rabbit.

IGOR: Now there's a hare-brained scheme!

Why can't the Frankenstein monster run a marathon?

He always ends up with a stitch in his side.

What did the girl monster say to the Frankenstein monster?

"You can be frank with me."

Why did Dr. Frankenstein use lightning to bring his monster to life?

He had to cut down on his electric bill.

What would you get if you crossed a frog with Dr. Frankenstein?

A hopping mad scientist.

What do you call it when Dracula, Frankenstein, the Wolfman and Igor all play golf together?

A fearsome foursome.

What's the tallest building in Transylvania?

The Vampire State Building.

Dracula is a sucker for a pretty neck.

Why did Count Dracula try out for the Olympic team?
He wanted to win a ghoul medal.

What track and field feat did the ghoul perform at the Monster Olympics?
A cemetery vault.

How do you measure a cemetery?
Use a graveyard stick.

Knock-Knock!
  Who's there?
Grave.
  Grave who?
Grave-y Crockett.

What dreaded disease do gravediggers get?
Bury-Bury!

What did the Wolfman umpire shout as the lady vampire flew away?
Bat-her-up!

Where do monsters go on fishing trips?
To Lake Eerie.

Knock-Knock!
  Who's there?
Devotion.
  Devotion who?
Devotion is the body of water Jaws swims in.

What monstrous armored vehicle did a mad scientist create?

Tankenstein.

When does King Kong get out on the dance floor?

When it's time to lead a Kong-a line.

What letter of the alphabet is secretly a monster?

The evil I.

What phone number should you dial when you see a monster coming toward you?

9-Run-Run!

What does the Invisible Man put in his coffee?
  Vanishing cream.

What does the Abominable Snowman put in his coffee?
  Cold cream.

How does Dracula drink his coffee?
  Regular. He doesn't care if it keeps him awake all night.

GIRL VAMPIRE: I just went out on a date with the Invisible Man.

GIRL WEREWOLF: I'll never understand what you see in that guy.

What would you get if you crossed a giant monster lizard with sour pickle juice?

Goddilla.

Why won't Godzilla eat an aircraft carrier?

He doesn't like food that has flies buzzing around it.

What would you get if you crossed Godzilla with a parrot?

I don't know, but when it spoke everyone would listen.

What looks like Dracula and floats in the ocean?

A bat buoy.

Why did the cowardly vampire go hungry?

It couldn't stand the sight of blood.

DRACULA: Tonight there's a full moon. Tomorrow there isn't.

WOLFMAN: Oh well, hair today, gone tomorrow.

"I was just bitten by a flying vampire."

"Now that's a stroke of bat luck!"

MAD SCIENTIST: Lift up that two ton baseball.

MONSTER: Ugh! I can't.

MAD SCIENTIST: You lifted it easily enough last Saturday.

MONSTER: I know, but today must be a weak day.

Who was the monster's favorite cheerleader?
Elvira-rah-rah, mistress of the dark.

What movie stars a moose and a squirrel?
Bullwinkle and Rocky Horror Picture Show.

What is the favorite monster movie of baseball players?
The Rocky Horror Pitcher Show.

Who is the sickest evil doctor in Asia?
Flu Manchu.

7. LAUGH ATTACKS

How do you keep a mummy crisp and fresh?
Use plastic wrap.

What did the little Egyptian boy say to the bully?
"Let me alone or I'll tell my mummy."

Why do mummies feel financially secure?
They buy lots of afterlife insurance.

What did the mummy crook say to the Egyptian detectives?

"You can't pin this wrap on me."

What would you get if you crossed a staircase with an ancient Egyptian?

A step mummy.

Knock-Knock!
   Who's there?
Egypt.
   Egypt who?
Egypt me when he sold me this used mummy case.

What did the werewolf say to the alphabet?
I came to eat U.

What happens when Frankenstein owns a butcher shop and has the Wolfman for a customer?
Frankenstein meats the Wolfman.

How do we know the Wolfman comes from a strange family?
He has one maw and four paws.

What do you call two vampires who have the same mother?
Blood brothers.

HORROR FILM DIRECTOR: Okay, Count Dracula. Change into a giant bat.
DRACULA: I don't know how.
HORROR FILM DIRECTOR: Well, just wing it.

Where does Dracula go when classes start?
Bat-to-school.

What do you put in a vampire's flashlight?
Batteries.

Why did the bat go into the cave?
It wanted to hang out with its pals.

Why did Dracula's girlfriend break up with him?
Because he stayed out late every night.

Where did Count Dracula go to college?
Bite U.

Why did Count Dracula bite a lightbulb?
He wanted brighter teeth.

Why is Dracula like false teeth?
They both come out at night.

Knock-Knock!
  Who's there?
I Ben.
  I Ben who?
I Ben a vampire for over 100 years.

What does Count Dracula wear over his pajamas?
A bat-robe.

Why was the vampire so poor?
It couldn't earn a day's pay.

How does Count Dracula design a computer?
Byte-by-byte.

How does Count Dracula travel over water?
In a blood vessel.

Where is the most dangerous place to live in
Transylvania?
Necks-door to Count Dracula.

CRAZY QUOTES FROM THE INVISIBLE MAN

My conscience is clear and so is the rest of me.

What you don't see is what you get.

No, you won't be seeing me later.

I don't care what you think—I am not a big nothing.

What plant only grows when it's dark out?
A night stalker.

What's creepy, green and grows in the jungle?
The Frankenvine Monster.

MONSTER: Relax, Doc. I'll finish sewing myself up.
MAD DOCTOR: Suture self.

Knock-Knock!

  Who's there?

Dewey.

  Dewey who?

Dewey have to watch horror movies again?

Knock-Knock!

  Who's there?

Lotta.

  Lotta who?

Lotta people are afraid of horror movies.

What ailment do dragons have on Valentine's Day?
Heartburn.

Knock-Knock!
  Who's there?
Dragon.
  Dragon who?
Dragon your feet dirties your shoes.

Knock-Knock!
  Who's there?
Logan.
  Logan who?
Logan see if there are any
monsters in the basement.

Knock-Knock!
  Who's there?
Wail.
  Wail who?
Wail hunt that vampire until we catch him.

Knock-Knock!
  Who's there?
Weird.
  Weird who?
Weird you put the silver bullet?

What does Mothra hit with a golf club?
Mothballs.

Where did Cinderella Mothra go?
  To the mothball.

Why did the latest Frankenstein monster keep burping?
  It was the new gas-powered model.

IGOR: What do I need to become your assistant?
MAD DOCTOR: A high ghoul diploma.

What did the policeman shout when he saw Dr. Frankenstein with a bunch of monsters?
  Hey, you—give me the creeps!

8. WHAT A SCREAM!

Why don't skeletons host T.V. talk shows?
   Because they have no body to talk with.

What monster is on a T.V. talk show?
   The Phantom of the Oprah.

Why was the goblin's phone bill so high?
   He made a lot of troll calls.

What was the fastest prehistoric monster?
The Prontosaurus.

What prehistoric monster does Dracula fear the most?
The Stakesaurus.

What jewel does Mrs. Zombie's wedding ring have in it?
A tombstone.

Knock-Knock!
   Who's there?
Karloff.
   Karloff who?
Karloff your dogs! I surrender.

Knock-Knock!
   Who's there?
Talon.
   Talon who?
Talon ghost stories can scare people.

Knock-Knock!
   Who's there?
Shepherd.
   Shepherd who?
Shepherd a monster outside, so Shep was afraid to
open the door.

Knock-Knock!
   Who's there?
I spider.
   I spider who?
I spider in the secret laboratory snooping around.

Knock-Knock!
   Who's there?
Kenny.
   Kenny who?
Kenny really bring that monster to life?

SINISTER SENTENCES

Ravenous—Thanks for ravenous to dinner.

Relic—Relic the icing off the cake.

Symmetry—Never go to a symmetry at night.

Sedate—I'll meet you at the Haunted House. Okay, sedate.

Poisonous—Poisonous and you'll go to jail.

What kind of pants did the monster wear?
  Boo-jeans.

What's hairy, scary, and slides down a snow-covered mountain really fast?

A Sasquatch on a snowboard.

How can you tell if a werewolf is an animal rights activist?

If it's an animal rights activist, it'll be wearing fake fur.

Which ghoul do waiters love?

Jack the Tipper.

MAD DOCTOR: Last night I created a horrible living rope monster.

BORIS: That's noose to me.

When does a mummy make stirfry vegetables?
When it woks up.

Did you hear about the architect who became a mad scientist?
Now he's a body builder.

IVAN: Why is your skeleton creature afraid to leave the laboratory?
MAD DOCTOR: Because it has no guts.

What candies do mad scientists eat after supper?
Experi-mints.

What would you get if you crossed Dracula with a clockmaker?

A night watchman.

What would you get if you crossed a space monster and a sea monster?

A Nep-tuna.

Why didn't the spaceship land in New York City?

Because it couldn't find a parking place.

How does a space monster hold up its pants?

With an asteroid belt.

What kind of spacecraft do ghosts fly?

Boo-F-Os.

Where did the space monster take the giant killer bee?

To a honeymoon.

What kind of music do space monsters like?

Moon rock and luna tunes.

How do you clean up a dirty space monster?

In a meteor shower.

What did the hungry space monster eat for lunch?

A satellite dish.

What creepy thing is found in Davy Jones' Locker?
The Combination Lock Ness Monster.

What does the Loch Ness Monster do when it wants
to borrow a book?
It uses a library cod.

What does the Loch Ness Monster do when it wants
to charge a purchase?
It uses a credit cod.

9. HORRIBLE HA-HA'S

What does a zombie use in the morning?
Aftergrave lotion.

Why did Mrs. Zombie join a monster exercise club?
So she could keep her ghoulish figure.

What car does the Bogey Man drive?
The Bogey Van.

Which monsters invented an airplane?
The Fright Brothers.

What ghost carries a pack and a rifle and goes on safari?
A big game haunter.

What monster helped win the American Civil War?
Ghoulysses S. Grant.

What would you get if you crossed a telephone with a vampire?
A ring-a-dingbat.

What picture did Leonardo paint after he saw a monster?

The Moaning Lisa.

What's the best way to talk to a monster?

Call it long distance.

Why did the space monster visit Rodan?

For a close encounter of the bird kind.

IVAN: Rodan, the giant bird monster, just had a baby.

IGOR: I bet it's a chirp off the old block.

What did Rodan say when the Concorde flew past?

"Oh, boy. Fast food for lunch!"

Which monster flew a kite during a thunderstorm?

Benjamin Franklinstein.

What scary monster lives in the mountains and is purple?

The Abominable Grapeman.

WOLFMAN: Who gave you that terrible scratch?

WEREWOLF: No one gave it to me. I had to fight for it.

Where does a traveling vampire stay while he's on the road?

At a cave inn.

What would you get if you crossed a Sasquatch with a centipede?

Big Foot-Foot-Foot-Foot. . . .

What happens when the Abominable Snowman punches Big Foot?

Big Foot is knocked cold.

What kind of pet does the Abominable Snowman have?

A chilly dog.

What do monsters do in cold weather?

Turn down the scare conditioner.

WEREWOLF: Is it dark out there?
VAMPIRE: I wouldn't know. I can't see a thing.

MOTHER: Eat your spinach. It'll put color in your cheeks.
BOY: What do I want with green cheeks?

What did the ghoul eat with his soup?

Dread and butter.

Why did the monster go into the clock shop?

It was trying to kill some time.

TEACHER: Use the word "graduate" in a sentence.
MONSTER STUDENT: Tell me, Wolf, are you graduate Little Red Riding Hood?

TEACHER: Use the word "burial" in a sentence.
MONSTER STUDENT: I feel burial today, so please call the doctor.

Why did the Wolfman go to a psychologist?
He had claws-trophobia.

How did the Wolfman move his family to Transylvania?
He rented a U-Howl Truck.

Where do you go to gas up a monster truck?
To a villain station.

Knock-Knock!
  Who's there?
Bella.
  Bella who?
Bella out of order.

How do monster dogs get from place to place?
They take the Greyhound bus.

MONSTER: I have a ringing in my head. Can you
  remove it?
DOCTOR: I'm a surgeon, not a phone operator.

What would you get if you crossed a werewolf with a vampire bat?

I don't know, but the fur would begin to fly.

DADDY MONSTER: This is a story about a werewolf.
LITTLE MONSTER: Oh, great! A furry tale!

WHAT DO YOU CALL...

...a shovel that belongs to a goblin?

A ghoul tool.

...a steel drum used by a giant ape?

A king kong gong!

...ice cream named after the monster who devoured Tokyo?

Vanilla Godzilla!

...a vampire college social club?

A bat frat!

...two ancient Egyptian buddies buried in a tomb together?

Chummy mummies!

What would you get if you crossed a werewolf and a vampire?

A creature that turns into a werewolf when the sun rises.

What would you get if you crossed a huge bird monster with King Kong?

A giant chirp-monk.

Where did Bankenstein go to learn about his future?

To an automatic fortune-teller machine.

GREGOR: I just saw a ten-foot monster.

BORIS: Wow! That is unusual. Most monsters only have two feet.

10. KNOCK YOURSELF OUT

Knock-Knock!
  Who's there?
Account.
  Account who?
Account is what Dracula is.

Knock-Knock!
  Who's there?
Agape.
  Agape who?
Agape is what Dracula wears over his shoulders.

Knock-Knock!
  Who's there?
Doughnut.
  Doughnut who?
Doughnut let werewolves into your house.

Knock-Knock!
  Who's there?
Regard.
  Regard who?
Regard the castle from monster attacks.

Knock-Knock!
  Who's there?
Armand.
  Armand who?
Armand big trouble!

Knock-Knock!
Who's there?
Former.
Former who?
Former monsters showed up to join our scary group.

Knock-Knock!
Who's there?
I'm Gibbon.
I'm Gibbon who?
I'm Gibbon up reading ghost stories.

Knock-Knock!
Who's there?
Hiatus.
Hiatus who?
Hiatus lunch and now the Wolfman is mad at me.

Knock-Knock!
Who's there?
Voodoo.
Voodoo who?
Voodoo you think is scarier,
Dracula or the Wolfman?

Knock-Knock!
Who's there?
It's a waffle.
It's a waffle who?
It's a waffle sight to see a monster standing on your porch.

Knock-Knock!
  Who's there?
I'm Cher.
  I'm Cher who?
I'm Cher afraid of werewolves.

Knock-Knock!
  Who's there?
Menu.
  Menu who?
Menu see a vampire, protect your neck.

Knock-Knock!
  Who's there?
Barn.
  Barn who?
Barn down Dracula's castle before he gets home.

Knock-Knock!
  Who's there?
Hour.
  Hour who?
Hour you going to destroy that vampire?

Knock-Knock!
  Who's there?
Turnip.
  Turnip who?
Turnip the voltage or we'll never bring this monster
to life.

Knock-Knock!
Who's there?
C.D.
C.D. who?
C.D. monster out here with me? Open up or he'll break down the door.

Knock-Knock!
Who's there?
Candice.
Candice who?
Candice zombie be brought back to life?

Knock-Knock!
Who's there?
Freeze.
Freeze who?
Freeze a jolly good fellow, even if he is a yeti.

Knock-Knock!
  Who's there?
Ewell.
  Ewell who?
Ewell be sorry if you move to Transylvania.

Knock-Knock!
  Who's there?
Design.
  Design who?
Design said beware of monsters.

Knock-Knock!
  Who's there?
Cement.
  Cement who?
Cement to scream when she saw Dracula, but she
fainted instead.

Knock-Knock!
  Who's there?
Revue.
  Revue who?
Revue making monsters as a serious crime.

Knock-Knock!
  Who's there?
Ooze.
  Ooze who?
Ooze monster is that on the operating table?

Knock-Knock!
  Who's there?
Rainy.
  Rainy who?
Rainy wakes up, tell him he was hypnotized.

Knock-Knock!
  Who's there?
Soil.
  Soil who?
Soil see you later at the Halloween party.

Knock-Knock!
  Who's there?
Dirge.
  Dirge who?
Dirge monsters in them there hills!

Knock-Knock!
  Who's there?
Wheelbarrow.
  Wheelbarrow who?
Wheelbarrow your garlic to protect us from the
vampire.

Knock-Knock!
    Who's there?
Zealous.
    Zealous who?
Zealous an amulet to protect us from monsters.

Knock-Knock!
    Who's there?
Weaver.
    Weaver who?
Weaver alone, you big bad monster. She's not
bothering you.

Knock-Knock!
    Who's there?
Welcome.
    Welcome who?
Welcome to your Halloween party if it's not too
scary.

Knock-Knock!
    Who's there?
I'm Gladys.
    I'm Gladys who?
I'm Gladys Halloween.

Knock-Knock!
    Who's there?
Fright.
    Fright who?
Fright—fright—fright for old Notre Dame!

Knock-Knock!
   Who's there?
Ah-choo!
   Ah-choo who?
"Ah-choo on people's necks," admitted Count Dracula.

Knock-Knock!
   Who's there?
Attila.
   Attila who?
Attila you again—stay out of the dungeon!

Knock-Knock!
   Who's there?
Eerie.
   Eerie who?
Eerie goes loob-y loo...

Knock-Knock!
   Who's there?
Sheena.
   Sheena who?
Sheena monster around here lately?

Knock-Knock!
   Who's there?
Zelda.
   Zelda who?
Zelda house. It's haunted.

11. WRAPPING IT UP

What quiz game do mummies like to play?
  Name that Tomb.

What did the horror flick director shout when his crew finished making a mummy movie?
  That's a wrap!

Which mummy has a static problem with his wrappings?
  Cling Tut.

What kind of candies does a mummy eat after dinner?
Parch-mints.

Why was the mummy so hungry?
He had a tape worm.

Which mummy was a football player?
King Hut-Hut-Hut!

What did the pharaoh say to the mummy?
Don't just lie there, shriek to me.

Why didn't the Invisible Girl buy the dress?
It was she-through.

The Invisible Man is not a See-Monster.

MAD DOCTOR: I just created a monster out of rubber bands.
IGOR: Was it a difficult operation?
MAD DOCTOR: Nah! It was a snap.

What monster is a space explorer?
Flash Gorgon.

What did Dracula say to his dog when he went out for the evening?

"Night Spot."

What kind of fir trees grow in Transylvania?

Frankenpines.

BORIS: I know a girl named Wanda who can cast spells.

IGOR: Oh—a magic Wanda!

How do we know the Loch Ness Monster is female?

Because everyone says she's a she-serpent.

What do Rodan and Mothra read at the breakfast table?

The flypaper.

What do you call it when Mothra fights other moths?

A moth brawl.

What would you get if you crossed the Wolfman with King Kong?

I don't know, but I don't want to be around when the full moon rises!

Knock-Knock!
   Who's there?
Hubie.
   Hubie who?
Hubie home before dark!

Knock-Knock!
Who's there?
Major.
Major who?
Major monster perform some tricks
while you were gone.

What would you get if you crossed the Abominable
Snowman with Rodan?
Cold and flew symptoms.

What is the Abominable Snowman's favorite pasta?
Spagh-yeti.

What is the Abominable Snowkid's favorite book?
The Blizzard of Oz.

What bug showed up at the Abominable
Snowman's picnic?
Ant-arctica.

Where did the Abominable Snowman keep his
secret money?
In a slush fund.

What is the Abominable Snowman's favorite
saying?
Have an ice day!

INDEX